REJECTION'S
BABY

IDENTIFYING AND ADDRESSING
UNRESOLVED REJECTION AND
WHAT IT GIVES BIRTH TO

YVETTE D. THOROUGHGOOD

Book Cover Design: Prize Publishing House

Printed by: Prize Publishing House, LLC in the United States of America.

First printing edition 2023.

Prize Publishing House
P.O. Box 9856, Chesapeake, VA 23321
www.PrizePublishingHouse.com

ISBN (Paperback): 979-8-9875046-0-4
ISBN (E-Book): 979-8-9875046-1-1

CONTENTS

INTRODUCTION

Rejection. Is it really that serious? Everyone, at some point, has dealt with rejection. It is a part of life.

According to the Merriam-Webster Dictionary, the definition of rejection is to refuse to accept, consider, submit to, take for some purpose, or use; to refuse to hear, receive, or admit; to spew out; to cast off.

Some of our first memories may include not being picked for the kickball team at recess or our crush not feeling the same way as we felt about them. However, there are forms of rejection that leave an emotional scar; and can cause one to carry a stigma. For instance, a child in the womb whose mother does not want them is born knowing they were rejected before birth. A child continuously bullied in school and lacking love and affection at home may also carry rejection into adulthood. Unfortunately, some had horror stories of molestation at the hands of an authority figure. Once the predator fulfilled a sick desire, there was no more use for the injured party. There are those who, through no fault of their own, had no relationship or a very bad one with their mother or father. Divorce, teenage pregnancy, and low socio-economic status are experiences that, if swept under the rug, can birth "unhealthy children." I do not speak of a tiny, precious gift of a human being that is born. Instead, I speak of a proverbial baby in the form of issues and stigmas that grow and fester over time.

CHAPTER 1
WHEN REJECTION GIVES BIRTH

There is an insecurity that comes with the spirit of rejection. If a person does not overcome this with the help of God, this individual becomes their own helper and finds a need to control or manipulate every environment they enter. When a person has been the victim and never wants to experience this again, **control becomes their drug.** When one has been made to feel pushed aside and out of control, control becomes the objective. The person can take on a spirit of rebellion. All the while, an unhealthy spirit is developing. **The offspring of rejection and rebellion is Witchcraft.**

"For rebellion is as the sin of Witchcraft, and stubbornness is as iniquity and idolatry. Because thou hast rejected the word of the Lord, he hath also rejected thee from being king." (1 Samuel 15:23, KJV)

Jezebel and the Spirit of Witchcraft

Jezebel was the daughter of Ethobaal, a Phoenician king, and the wife of King Ahab, who ruled the kingdom of Israel. When Jezebel married Ahab, she influenced him to worship Baal, a nature god. They worshipped not only Baal but also Ashtoreth, his female counterpart. As a woman seeking more power, she sought to destroy those who questioned her, and most of the prophets of God were murdered at her request.

Although Jezebel was a woman, the spirit in which she operated was not gender-specific. Before we go any further, her name means "unexalted one." Another translation of her name includes the word "dung," which also translates as *refuse* or *reject*. There is not much to be said about Jezebel's mother, which also raises another red flag. Who did she have to nurture her? Who taught her what a young lady should know? Did she ever know her mother? Did her mother have a voice in their home? It is said that Jezebel was raised with the finest and received a good education, but her home life lacked love, and her father rejected her. The only feminine influence we read of regarding Jezebel is the pagan goddess Ashtoreth. We will further explore this character later on.

Jezebel was joined in marriage to Ahab as a sign of a political alliance between their fathers.

Ahab was double-minded and would toil between righteousness and evil. He had more of a reputation for working evil. The Bible says, "And Ahab the son of Omri did evil in the sight of the LORD above all that *were* before him." (1 Kings 16:30, KJV)

He promoted Baal and Ashtoreth worship, homosexuality, bestiality, and prostitutes in the temple of God.

He was double-minded, so, therefore, it gave room to Jezebel to seduce him into doing all manner of evil to keep her on top. After rebellion and rejection consummate their union, the goal was ALWAYS to control. You might ask, "Well, why would anyone grant this spirit access?" Because it is cunning, manipulative, seducing, and deceptive.

Witchcraft is a religious practice involving magic and affinity with nature, usually within a pagan tradition, bewitching or fascinating attraction or charm.

If you have ever done any research on cults, Witchcraft is in full operation. The leader isolates, manipulates, and intimidates their followers.

What does this look or sound like?

Isolation: *"Your family doesn't understand you." "We're the only ones who love you." "Don't listen to any ministers or read any books if we have not approved them."*

Manipulation: *"Obey your leader; you must do WHATEVER I SAY."*

Intimidation: *"If you don't sow XXXX.00, God won't bless you. I don't care if it is your bill money."*

Witchcraft is also a spirit that DESPISES authority. It will mask itself as help or support to authority figures. The goal is to learn the ingredients of the "secret sauce."

A person who operates in this way stays around long enough to sniff out the weaknesses in a leader or organization. They then step in and "save the day." Their foot is in the door, and they can obtain the authority and respect they initially sought.

This spirit can only dominate when we are out of our places. This happens in ministry, family circles, and the workplace. When we become passive in our assignments, we leave the "porchlight on and the door unlocked" to this spirit.

When we have people in our lives who operate in this spirit, we must not become complicit in their workings. We cannot cloak or cover; it must be addressed.

Double-mindedness begins with rejection and opens the door to an unstable identity and personality. Here are some signs and symptoms that a person may have a spirit of rejection:

- A constant desire for physical love and assurance of self-worth
- Addiction
- Attention seeking
- Despair
- Despondency
- Discouragement
- Envy
- Fears Frustration
- Guilt
- Hopelessness
- Impatience
- Inferiority
- Inordinate affection for animals
- Loneliness
- Lust

- Perverseness
- Pride
- Revenge
- Self-rejection
- Sensitivity
- Shame
- Suicide/Suicidal ideation
- Unworthiness
- Vanity
- Withdrawal

This should not be ignored when you consistently see these characteristics/symptoms operating in an individual or yourself. Pray for and encourage Godly counsel.

_____

_____

_____

_____

_____

_____

_____

_____

_____

_____

_____

CHAPTER 2
THE DRIVING
FORCE BEHIND
THIS SPIRIT

Jezebel served idol gods. She was most devoted to Ashtoreth (also called Asherah, Ashtereth, and the groves – 1 Kings 14:23; 1 Kings 16:30-34). Ashtoreth was the goddess of war, fertility, the sun, and the moon. The sun and the moon portion of her "deity" are closely related to astrology. Some psychics and people operate in the spirit of Witchcraft and can give you a "prophecy" and be spot on! They "prophesy" according to the stars. They operate in a pseudo-anointing. The spirit of Ashtoreth is the driving force behind the Witchcraft spirit. It attempts to duplicate the things of God to fool the people of God. People in the house of God who operate in this spirit have a "form of godliness, but deny the power thereof: from such turn away." (2 Timothy 3:5, KJV)

One of Ashtoreth's manifestations is the **Atar-gatis** – the torso of a woman with the tail of a fish. How does this relate? There is a species of fish called *Anthias.* If the male Anthias isn't aggressive enough, the most dominant female will begin to change its sex into a male. Like the fish, when Ashtoreth senses weakness in any authority figure, she automatically assumes authority. In the same manner, Jezebel would override her husband when she felt he was being weak.

In 1 Kings 21, beginning in verse four, Ahab returns home upset because he wants to buy a vineyard from a man named Naboth, and it didn't go his way. Naboth declines the offer because it is his inheritance. Jezebel starts to pump him up, saying, "Aren't you the governor of the kingdom of Israel?" She tells him to change his countenance and that **she** will get it for him. She wrote letters in Ahab's name, proclaimed a fast, had some men set Naboth up, then had him stoned to death. When she heard Naboth was dead, she told Ahab, "Go get your vineyard." That spirit will find out what a leader or "love interest" wants and obtain it by any means necessary to gain control. You see this in romantic relationships, government, corporate America, and the Church. This spirit can gain access through the leader's permission because it is deceptive. It does not operate in love or compassion. It is very cold and aloof and only "cozies up" to the leader/authority figure. You will not see this individual acclimate to the environment; the objective is to control the environment.

Always remember, the motive is never for the greater good, but the motive is total domination.

CHAPTER 3
THE NEED FOR CONTROL

When Control Becomes an Addiction

Many times when an individual walks in unresolved re-jection, control is like a drug. It is almost as if they have entered an unspoken contract that says they will never be ignored, rejected, or mishandled again.

Let's go through a scenario. I'll preface this scenario with this statement: the goal is not to antagonize a person who operates in this spirit; but to identify and adequately address the spirit. We'll call the main character Salina. As a child, Salina's mother chose men over her. Salina found herself in situations where she was neglected and abused by her mother. She was picked on in school and always felt over-looked. She joins the military after high school and attends a church on base. She hears the Gospel and believes that God can change her life. She prays the prayer of salvation, starts going to Bible Study, and becomes very active in the min-istry. The issue is she never surrenders the rejection. She has major walls, many defense mechanisms, and walks in the spirit of offense. She did not have a good relationship with her mom, so she didn't give any female authority figure a chance. She aims to highjack their role and "show them how it's done." This follows her post-military. There is an ulterior motive in every job, club, and ministry she joins. She seeks out smaller congregations that are a bit unorganized because the pastors/leaders are usually worn out and are praying for help. Salina always shows up disguised as the help that is needed. She does not bond with the members of the organization but goes straight to the leader with a portfolio of her gifts and accomplishments. I have to pause right here. This is an individual who operates in the spirit of rebellion or Witchcraft. This spirit is not gender-specific; however, it is primarily seen in women. Whether it be a job, church, club, or government, a Salina will target organizations where help is scarce; this is how one gains access to confidential information and the ear of the leadership. Control is like a drug, and an individual who operates in this spirit will work past exhaustion with the goal of total domination.

If you work in your church, it is essential never to leave your commitment uncovered. It is as though that spirit has a radar for ministries or organizations that do not operate in the spirit of excellence.

This spirit has mastered the art of being a chameleon. It knows how to put on a front like it's concerned. It tries to master every function in its environment and becomes extremely "helpful."

This is not to say that every person who comes to your church to help is operating in the spirit of Witchcraft. What should be taken from this is, *don't be in haste to appoint new partners/members in leadership positions or roles where they are privy to confidential information (e.g., finance, pastor's armorbearer).*

_____

_____

_____

_____

_____

_____

_____

_____

_____

_____

_____

_____

CHAPTER 4
MANIPULATION –
A SURE SIGN
OF REJECTION

Manipulation is a behavior designed to exploit, control, or harmfully influence to one's advantage. Manipulators can be very cunning. People who have issues with rejection sometimes learn to maneuver through life and maintain control by using manipulative tactics. It becomes second nature to the point where they would never label it as such.

A few signs of manipulation are guilt-tripping, using monetary or material things to gain someone's loyalty, and lying.

The act of guilt–tripping is an attempt of the manipulator to sit in the "victim's seat." If you find an individual constantly using guilt to coerce you into conforming to what they desire, pay close attention. You should not feel constant guilt or as though you have done someone wrong when dealing with a loved one. Guilt-tripping will have you questioning yourself and apologizing when you haven't done anything that requires an apology. Anyone who always plays the victim will one day paint you as the perpetrator. Be very careful and do not fall into this trap. Don't become loyal to the point of your own detriment.

Using monetary or material things to "buy" someone's affection is a clear sign of manipulation. Gifts are nice, but if an individual is of little value to you without the nice gifts, it's not a genuine connection. You'll notice that once you do something that angers the individual, the gifts will stop, or they will remind you of what they have done for you.

A person who lies is fearful. One might lie to appear impressive so they can spark or keep your interest. A narcissistic romantic partner may cheat on you and then project as though you are cheating to get the focus off them.

Manipulation becomes a survival tactic and a way of life for some.

Your love or acceptance will not change a person who exhibits these behaviors. They must admit there is a problem and at least want to get to the root of it. Prayer and therapy are important in these situations.

Manipulation is a characteristic of Witchcraft. Witchcraft is about control. Manipulation is a tactic to control your mind and isolate you from anyone you deeply esteem or love. The individual who manipulates desires to be the "end-all." They will feel threatened by anyone else whom you highly regard. Their next move is to sow discord among you and your loved ones. They will work hard to convince you that they are the only person who truly loves you and that you absolutely need them.

When this type of relationship has run its course, its end is usually very messy. It's important to be proactive. Take time to evaluate your circle every so often. Don't ignore red flags, and don't sweep matters of concern under the rug, for they will surely show up again.

CHAPTER 5
PEOPLE OVER
POWER

If you are reading this book, I am confident you have unique gifts and talents. Ephesians 2:10 tells us, " For we are his workmanship, created in Christ Jesus for good works, which God prepared beforehand, that we should walk in them." If you notice, there is no prejudice or partiality implied. It does not say, "We men," "We women," or "We Black, White or Asian." That we includes you! We are God's workmanship. God created us and takes joy in loving what He made, as an artist would look at his priceless painting, as a sculptor would stand back and admire a beautiful, sculpted piece, skillfully created with his own hands. This is only a frail comparison because God delights in us so much more.

He made us, not as an extra or a plan B. But before our father knew our mother, God had a plan to design us for great things, to impact generations. Any gift given to us by God is intended to help others. Our gifts were never meant to make us arrogant, high-minded, or lofty. When did we get to the place where we loved power more than people? When did we arrive at "Prove A Point Central?"

Many fall in love with power when they have been made to feel powerless. That powerlessness is seeded in rejection. People in positions of authority do sometimes abuse their power.

There are parents, CEOs, spiritual leaders, spouses, and the list goes on of people who operate as narcissists. *What is a narcissist?* A narcissist is someone who has an excessive interest in or admiration of themselves and believes that the world should revolve around them. A narcissist tends to be egocentric – which is a self-centered state of mind and an attitude that views other values and points of view as subordinate.

Their behaviors can have a damaging effect on the person for whom their will was imposed. Having a point to prove is often birthed out of rejection. Some are fine without the invitation to join the "in crowd." Others internalize this as though they have an inadequacy. So time is wasted trying to prove to others why one is "good enough." When we allow this to happen, we lose sight of the mission because we focus on our misery. A ministry should be birthed out of what was intended to make you miserable. There is such a thing as learning what *not* to do. When you've been in a place where you were not accepted, it should only make you more conscious that you're not providing someone else with that same experience.

We rob ourselves of rich experiences and relationships when we value power more than the people we were called to help.

This can bring on a strong spirit of unhealthy competition. We can operate in what some describe as "the spirit of excellence;" however, competition robs you of your compassion. People know when you care. They may not say it, but they see it.

CHAPTER 6
WORD CURSES

There are Christians who don't believe that word curses exist; oh, but they do. A person with a green face, a hat, and a broom is not the source of this. If anyone has ever said, "You will never amount to anything," "You're not smart enough," or "You'll never be successful," these are forms of word curses. Words have power! They do not always take root. But when you have a place of vulnerability in the area where the curse was spoken, sometimes you will experience residue from the curse that was spoken. This is why you should bathe your mind in the word of God. Think on things that are "honest, pure, lovely and of a good report" (Philippians 4:8, KJV). All too often, negativity is spoken over our lives when we are not present. Stay in the will and word of God, and the weapons may form but will not prosper.

A word curse was spoken over the prophet Elijah when he slayed the prophets of Baal (1 Kings 18). Elijah slayed 850 prophets of Baal, which was huge. After this occurred, he felt vulnerable. Remember Jezebel defies authority and wants ultimate domination. If this spirit operates through a woman, she can't stand real men. She is comfortable around eunuchs or a male who has been emasculated. So when she received word that Elijah slayed Baal's prophets, she became angry. Jezebel sent a messenger to Elijah, saying, "May the gods punish me terribly if by this time tomorrow I don't kill you just as you killed those prophets" (1 Kings 19:2). When Elijah heard this, he was afraid and ran for his life, taking his servant with him. Now, remember, he had just killed 850 prophets, but because he was vulnerable, he ran and hid.

We can become overwhelmed with our businesses, jobs, ministry assignments, and the list goes on. If we don't stop and refuel, our tank is empty. This is an opportune time for that spirit to strike. Remember, if you have given your life to the Lord, you are covered. This spirit will not get the advantage. However, at times in our vulnerability, we notice that things feel off or chaotic. Here are a few signs that someone is actively speaking word curses over you:

- Frequent car accidents
- A sickness that seems to "come out of nowhere," and the doctor can't figure it out
- Constant confusion in your close relationships

Just because you have experienced one of the above situations doesn't mean that it is a result of a word curse. If you notice a trend, turn up your warfare during your prayer time.

Cover your family and all that concerns you in prayer:

Lord Jesus, I thank You for Your kindness and Your protection. I break every word curse and diabolical plot formed against my family and all that concerns me. Let Your blood cover us; let Your blood prevail. I bind the spirit of death, and I loose life. I bind up the spirit of heaviness and I loose the joy of the Lord. I decree and declare that all things are working together for my good. In Jesus' name, amen.

Jealousy and Friendly Fire

It is important to discern the nature of your relationships. Know the difference between concealed jealousy and genuine love coming from a friend. We need to be very careful of whom we confide in. You've heard the song, "They smile in your face. All the while trying to take your place; Backstabbers!" You never want to give an enemy posing as a friend "inside information." You only widen the "target" on your back when you do so.

CHAPTER 7
REJECTION AND THE BODY

The effects of rejection can manifest physically. Unresolved rejection will not be ignored. It will rear its head in all types of ways. Research was recorded in a popular publication to prove that rejection can physically hurt. A neuroscientist proved that the brain does not experience emotional and physical pain the same; however, the same chemical is released during both events. It's safe to say that rejection is a blow to the body. Going about your everyday life without addressing rejection is like an injured player still trying to play in a game. The injury can worsen, affecting their effectiveness on the court.

Unresolved rejection can affect your cardiovascular system, pulmonary system, gastrointestinal system, and even your musculoskeletal system. Inflammation is associated with the diseases of these body systems.

There was a study done at UCLA. More than 100 healthy individuals underwent testing that would trigger social stress and rejection to see how certain areas of the brain would respond. There were inflammatory markers as well. The end result was that the parts of the brain associated with fear, rejection, and stress were lit, and the inflammation markers increased significantly after these tests were performed.

Have you ever heard someone tell someone they don't like, "You make me sick?" Turns out they weren't lying. If you've ever had a breakup with someone you love and didn't feel like yourself, it may have been the physical effects of rejection.

Not only can unhealed, unaddressed rejection impact your health, but it can hamper your potential and your purpose. Rejection affects your vision. Through rejection's lens, everyone is against you and you must compete with them until you dominate. Rejection's perception makes you think that another person's success is your direct enemy. Feelings of insecurity will allow you to think that constructive criticism is an attack on your character and ability.

Too often, we see public figures, influencers, and ministry leaders bleeding on people that did not injure them. This can also be viewed as a blow to the Body of Christ.

Pride is at the root of why individuals don't take the time to sit themselves down and be healed. It is important to understand that, if you are an individual people follow in any capacity, you bear a huge responsibility. Whatever spirit and attitude you operate in goes out to your audience. Their spirits and ears are opened to receive what you put out. Like a viral infection can spread through an audience like a fire, your influence can adversely affect those who admire you. If you feed on jealousy, envy, and negative thinking daily, you become toxic and are feeding your audience poison.

PEOPLE OF INFLUENCE – hear me, please. Operating in error to receive an honorarium or get "views" on social media is not worth it. If you are clear on your purpose and are sincere about fulfilling your God-given assignment, you can put pride aside and allow the healing to begin.

Yes, there are people who sing your praises and testify that you've helped them, but the impact is more significant when it's not done in a spirit of competition or rejection.

The tendency to want to "one-up" or prove a point is a symptom of rejection and a characteristic of pride.

It's okay to retreat to seek treatment and receive healing for the issue.

_____

_____

_____

_____

_____

_____

_____

_____

_____

_____

_____

CHAPTER 8

HOW DO WE BREAK THIS SPIRIT?

It must be exposed. If you operate in this spirit, you must cry out to God and repent. Then you must renounce (formally declare one's abandonment of) the spirit of Witchcraft and the very root of it. Ask God to fill or refill you with His precious Holy Ghost. Get in and stay in the word of God. Speak with your pastor or spiritual leader and ask for accountability. If you have nurtured rejection's baby for a while, it will look for a place to return. Do not underestimate the power of counseling to address deep seeded rejection.

If you are in a ministry or setting where this spirit is in operation, you must live holy and be consistent in your assignment. We have to cry holy, walk holy, talk holy! Consistency. Prayer warriors, pray for your leader and ministry so that every crack this spirit attempts to enter will be shut. Pray that the individual will receive deliverance.

In 2 Kings 9, Jehu confronts Jezebel with boldness and commands the Eunuchs to throw her down.

We must command that anything unlike the spirit of God is thrown down. If it's our friend or family member, it must be called out. We must avoid getting in a huddle and gossiping or cliquing up. We become a part of the problem when we do this. We must pray, fast, and hold up the arms of the leader. When we remove distractions, see them for what they are, and link together in warfare, God will change things, and the spirit will be broken.

PRAYERS

Prayer To Renounce the Spirit of Rejection

Dear Jesus, I come to You as humbly as I know how,
asking You to forgive me of all my sins. I also take
this time to break ties with the spirit of rejection.
It is a hindrance to my life and growth. I renounce
the spirit of rejection and all its ties in Jesus's name.
I break every spirit of bondage in Your presence.
I break the spirit of envy and any of its partners.
I renounce any ungodly covenant or illegal
agreement made by anyone in my bloodline.
I renounce the spirit of rebellion. I renounce the spirit of
manipulation, intimidation, and control in Jesus' name.
Lord Jesus, I receive Your freedom, power,
and victory at this very moment.
I thank You, Jesus, that satan's power
is broken in Your name. Amen.

A Prayer of Forgiveness

Father, in Jesus' name, I realize that Your word declares I must forgive to be forgiven. Please forgive me for holding grudges. I release *(fill in the name(s))* of any debt that I've held them responsible for. I forgive every person who misused, mishandled, or rejected me. I place them in Your care. I ask You, Heavenly Father, to heal my heart in Jesus' name. Amen.

The Prayer of Salvation

Lord Jesus, I am a sinner. Please forgive me for my sins. I believe that You died for my sins, rose, and are now seated at the right hand of God. Come into my heart, Lord Jesus. I confess You as my Lord and Savior. Thank You, Lord, for saving me.
In Jesus's name. Amen.

LET'S ASSESS

Take a moment to self-assess.

- Do I deal with unresolved rejection? *Go back as far as you remember and search yourself.*
- Do I struggle with jealousy when a friend or acquaintance accomplishes a goal before I do? If so, what do I say about this individual in my head? Do I downplay their accomplishment?
- Do I tend to become angry when my friends don't do what I want them to do? Does it irritate me when they don't think as I think? *Write about it.*
- What is your overall attitude toward authority figures? *Answer honestly, thinking about your current relationships or interactions with individuals in authority.*

Based on your answers, are there areas where healing is needed? If so, what will be your first step?

I celebrate you for taking the assessment and moving toward self-awareness. I pray something you've read has empowered or informed you.